Komiete Tetteh

3 Days in the Life of an Environmental Program Manager

A Reflection on the Identity Crisis in Planning and the link between Planning Theory and Practice

GRIN Verlag

Bibliografische Information der Deutschen Nationalbibliothek:

Die Deutsche Bibliothek verzeichnet diese Publikation in der Deutschen National-bibliografie; detaillierte bibliografische Daten sind im Internet über http://dnb.d-nb.de/ abrufbar.

Imprint:

Copyright © 2013 GRIN Verlag GmbH
Druck und Bindung: Books on Demand GmbH, Norderstedt Germany
ISBN: 978-3-656-57376-0

This book at GRIN:

http://www.grin.com/en/e-book/266640/3-days-in-the-life-of-an-environmental-program-manager

GRIN - Your knowledge has value

Der GRIN Verlag publiziert seit 1998 wissenschaftliche Arbeiten von Studenten, Hochschullehrern und anderen Akademikern als eBook und gedrucktes Buch. Die Verlagswebsite www.grin.com ist die ideale Plattform zur Veröffentlichung von Hausarbeiten, Abschlussarbeiten, wissenschaftlichen Aufsätzen, Dissertationen und Fachbüchern.

Visit us on the internet:

http://www.grin.com/

http://www.facebook.com/grincom

http://www.twitter.com/grin_com

3 DAYS IN THE LIFE OF AN ENVIRONMENTAL PROGRAM MANAGER:
A Reflection on the Identity Crisis in Planning and the link between Planning Theory and Practice

By
Komiete Tetteh

Abstract

This is a piece of writing that reflects on one of the current debates in the field of planning—the subject and profession of planning. I narrate how my three-day experience with a biologist working with community groups, corporate organizations and local governments to create and maintain dynamic urban green spaces in communities within the south-western Canadian province of British Columbia exposed my intellectual naivety about the very profession I am aspiring to become. My critical assessment of the contributions of the environmentalist, who is without formal training in community development or social planning, to community-building and social mobilization through his environmental and climate change mitigation programs, as well as the manner in which he deals with the daily challenges he encounters, shows how appropriate a professional planning identity, if so cherished by him, would be legitimate and justifiable. Focusing on the questions of what planning is and what planners do, I judge this assertion by scrutinizing the activities, communication acts, knowledge and skill-base of the biologist, from both practical and theoretical lenses. My findings and analysis display planning's elusive notion of being a knowledge power house; show how change is effected at the grassroots; shed insight on the link between planning theory and practice; and offer some useful insights for those considering a profession in community development and social planning. Yet, I also note that while planning is increasingly becoming expansive, threatening its traditional identity and rendering it somewhat vague, its relevance and uniqueness remains unquestionable in our current world bedeviled by a complex maze of challenges of an unprecedented scale.

Key Words: Planning, planning theory, community development, environment, profession

1. Introduction

Compared with traditional occupations such as farming, medicine and law, which are closely connected with the early development of human civilizations, planning is a relatively young profession. Contemporary planning is said to have begun in the 1900s as concerns over appalling social conditions, including cram-med housing, disease spread, bad sanitation, pollution, social vices and ribbon development, in major European and American settlements in the aftermath of the industrial and agricultural revolutions turned into visible social move-ments. This resulted in the crafting of plans and legislative instruments based on the ideas of

1

thinkers such as Ebenezer Howard (of Great Britain) and Daniel Burhamm (of the USA) to promote the virtues of civic and moral order, as well as beauty, efficiency, beauty and harmony—values pioneered by the Garden City and City Beautiful movements which they respectively founded or joined (Hodge, 2005).

But this redemptive perspective of planning history, often described by its detractors as the "official story", is criticized for the enlightenment-driven interest (of material progress through scientific rationality) of its proponents; for the discriminatory and marginalizing effects of its practices; and for the cerebral and "white male-privileged" viewpoint of planning's past, to the utter disregard for other forms and accounts of planning, particularly by the victims of modernist planning, including women and minority communities, in mainstream planning historiography (Sandercook, 1998). Related to this is the contention about the subject of planning theory—the intellectual roots and ideological foundations that shape the profession in its contemporary form and practice.

In spite of these internal wranglings, however, planning has grown to become a major profession in our world today, giving birth to many sub-fields and obtruding almost every facet of society and field of human endeavor: from the way we run government, to the way we grow the economy; from the way we manage environmental challenges, to the way we deal with exclusion; from the way promote equity, to the way we battle exploitation; from the way we encourage change, to the way we maintain standard practices; from the way we interpret knowledge to the way we influence outcomes; and from the way understand problems to the way we communicate solutions, making it challenging to provide a singular definition of what planning is and who planners are. Unsurprisingly, therefore, planners everywhere have difficulty explaining who they are, what they do, where they come from, and where they are going. Yet, as a relatively young profession grappling to establish a legitimate and enduring professional identify for itself, planning must find ways to approach these challenges.

In this paper, I reflect on the problem of identity in planning as featured in the current thinking and debate on the professional landscape. I do so by drawing on excerpts from an eight-hour period I spent over three days with the manager of *Common Grounds* Program at Evergreen Vancouver, an environmental non-profit organization, in the Fall of 2008. I realize that, judging from a practical point of view as well as the requisite intellectual capacity and skills, there are perhaps many more people engaged in various forms of planning work who have not necessarily sat under the tutelage of planning institutions than those recognized in official circles. These professionals, who come from diverse disciplinary backgrounds and posses varying degrees of educational attainment, apply a wide array of skills and knowledge, some of which are inborn, while others are acquired through formal training and experiential learning. Yet, their contribution to development is as significant as professionally trained planners.

2

I prove this by examining the nature of the work done by the program manager in question; the types of knowledge he brings to bear in his profession; the forms of value, skills and talents he exhibits through his activities; the kinds of people, places and institutions he interacts with; the nature of problems he encounters; and the methods he employs in dealing with them. I then reflect on the mix of planning theories implicit in his actions and conduct. In the immediate section that follows, I narrate my three-day encounter with the environmentalist, including what led me to embark on the exercise and how my experience with him unfolded. The first episode is from a workshop he facilitated; the second and the third are from his regular work days at the office, but present different events. My thoughts on why I think my interviewee could rightfully be regarded as a planner, judging from my observations about his work and actions and their relationship to planning theory, is offered after the accounts in section three. The implications for the planning profession of my observations from my encounter with the professional in question are highlighted in section four.

2. Encounters with an Environmental Steward
Day 1: Thursday November 27, 2008
Administering a Complementary Political Interest

Walking swiftly, I look at my time, and it's 3:27pm (local time) in Vancouver. I finally arrive at the premises of the Central Area Office of the Greater Vancouver Regional Government in central Burnaby, British Columbia, Canada, where a workshop is underway. I am not exactly sure of the purpose of this gathering: who is attending, what is being discussed, or how it is even going to benefit me. But on reaching the entrance to this beautiful-looking structure, flanked by a huge expanse of woods, I heave a sigh of relief, as I finally have the opportunity to meet for the first time the gentleman I am desperately looking for.

Flipping open the door, I see a hanging with the caption "Evergreen-Trees for Tomorrow Workshop", and this gives my wondering mind an idea, blurred though, of what this meeting is about. Anyhow, I keenly follow the direction given me by the receptionist to the seminar room where the event is on-going. Gently turning the knob I see a small attentive audience sitting around a conference table meticulously listening to a gentleman supposedly speaking to them about an important issue, aided by a PowerPoint. Responding gleefully to the welcome gesture from an onlooking participant, who spots me while slipping in, I take a seat and fervidly switch my mind from roving about all the troubles I had encountered while making my way to this rather thorny location, to focus on the subject of the meeting.

Unknown to me initially, Mr. Tim Part[1], who is the reason for my presence in the room, is the very person doing the presentation. Tim had invited me to attend the event after several weeks, if not months, of telephone conversations, in which I had been talking to, and persuading, him about my intention to drop shadow on him

---

[1] This is a pseudonym I'm using in order to protect the personal identity of my interviewee.

3

for a Planner's Day assignment. This assignment I make mention of is essentially a requirement for a planning history and theory course I am taking at one of north America's oldest planning schools, the University of British Columbia— an institution whose year of establishment parallels that of the emergence of the theoretical foundations of the very profession it seeks to train students in.

Adopting a partly historical and partly thematic approach, the class had been looking at the main intellectual movements of the last two hundred years as they relate to the emergence of planning, and discussing how these ideas have contributed to shaping the profession in its form and practice today. Our examination of the different perspectives and accounts of the history of planning shows diverse and sometimes conflicting views about the subject of planning history and theory; nevertheless, it reveals their importance to practice.

To help students further deepen their appreciation of the complex, yet inescapable, relationship between theory and practice in connection to this growing field, the course instructor (a planning theorist herself) asked students to spend a day with a planner working within the city or province where the university is located, to observe the nature of their daily work, while reflecting on the type of knowledge, skills and theories imbedded in their actions and professional approach in their field of practice.

My host Tim Part is a biologist, not a planner, so you can rightly question my decision to shadow

him and also appreciate his initial hesitation in endorsing my request, which you will soon get to know. But upon further persuasion and clarification of the academic intent of my assignment, Tim finally accepts my request and, in turn, invites me to attend this event, without giving me a hint that he is making the presentation. And on this premise, I, with critical lens and ears, begin to look, listen and observe his every action and word carefully in order to make sense of what is going on.

Apparently, Mr. Part and his project team from Evergreen, the organization they work for, are conducting a public education and information workshop—the third of twenty-five such workshops slated for a new program Evergreen has partnered the Government of the Canadian province of British Columbia to undertake within the next five years. This program, titled "Trees for Tomorrow", is an environmental initiative meant to support the Province's climate change initiatives, whilst complementing the development of safe, healthy and green communities.

According to Mr. Part, the provincial government launched the $13 million scheme in 2008 to support communities in British Columbia (BC)—small and large, rural and urban—to address the environmental challenges they face while maximizing the values from their urban forests, through the planting of 4 million trees in public spaces, including schoolyards, hospital grounds, civic parks, campuses, and parking lots throughout BC over the next five years. The overarching goal of "Trees for Tomorrow", Tim elaborates, is: "to reduce greenhouse gases in the atmosphere by at least 33 per cent below current levels by 2020". He also explains that planting trees in urban areas will help lock away greenhouse gases that would otherwise contribute to climate change. According to him, this is a great opportunity for people to come together to make their communities greener, healthier, stronger and beautiful.

"Trees are indeed a critical part of our future, and Evergreen has been planting trees together with thousands of community groups, municipalities, students and home-owners across the province for almost two decades. We are very proud to be supporting the Province of British Columbia as it works to fulfill its vision to lead the world in sustainable environmental management", Tim adds.

Proceeding, Mr. Part takes his time to unpack the key components of the scheme, beginning with the program objectives, project streams, funding arrangements, application processes, and eligibility requirements. Concerning the program's objectives, he indicates that, in addition to the environmental aims, it also has some economic and social objectives that seek to enhance the wellbeing of the people of British Columbia, which he highlights as follows:

Environmental

1. To significantly increase BC's carbon sink through urban afforestation;
2. To expand urban forests, enabling local governments to meet their Climate Action Charter obligations;
3. To accelerate the forest regeneration of Mountain Pine Beetle affected urban areas; and

4. To contribute to achieving zero net deforestation policy;

Economic

1. To facilitate major investments in local tree nurseries through purchase of inventory; and
2. To contribute to energy savings in communities.

Social

1. To transform spaces into areas where residents can be physically and socially active;
2. To promote the value of urban afforestation through education and extension; and
3. To optimize the strategic and continued involvement of youth and other community organizations.

Taking time to explain each set of objectives and the connection between them helps Tim's audience to appreciate the linkages between the environment, economic growth and social development. For instance, through the purchase of seedlings from local nurseries, income and employment opportunities will be created for local residents; and through the activity of tree planting, members of a community—be it an institution or residential area—can interact, have fun and build relationships. Besides, the naturalized areas provide safe and healthy spaces for people in the community to gather, learn, relax and play, while deepening their connection with nature that acts as a balm for the human spirit. Environmentally, these green zones filter pollutants, moderate temperatures, provide food and shelter for wildlife, and at the same time release oxygen and nitrogen to suppress carbon dioxide in the atmosphere that causes climate change.

Touching on the range of projects covered under the scheme, Mr. Part explains that three major categories have been designed to engage all elements of society and to encourage environmentally-friendly choices by individuals, business and communities. The first is BC150 Groves, in which communities may plant BC150 groves (groves of trees planted as a BC150 legacy, which is to celebrate BC's 150th anniversary as a Crown Colony). The second is Community Tree Project, which involves the planting of trees (one to three gallon pots) in community and regional parks, boulevards, parking lots and other public spaces. And the third is Urban Mountain Pine Beetle Affected Area Renewal Project, which involves planting of one to two year-old seedlings in urban areas affected by the pine beetle epidemic.

"Trees for Tomorrow" is being implemented through a public-private partnership model involving cost-sharing with applicants. Thus, Tim goes ahead to explain the details of the funding arrangements to participants. The Province will fund up to 50% of a project, with a maximum amount of $50,000 per project to cover the costs of trees and shrubs, seedlings (in the case of urban Mountain Pine Beetle affected area renewal only), mulch, tree guards and mulch mats. The remainder of the total cost of the project, which include land acquisition, human resources and equipment, is to be borne by prospective applicants through partnerships with other stakeholders and may be provided in the form of cash, or in-kind support, or a combination of both. For example, a company may donate 300 native trees or a school may volunteer 50 youth for two hours each. These count as in-kind contributions from his explanation.

Eligible applicants for the grant, Mr. Part mentions, include local governments, First Nations, institutional landowners (for example, hospitals and universities), and school districts.

Reviewing the application process and eligibility requirements for successful projects, Mr. Part stresses the need for applicants to develop a comprehensive project and site plan that outlines goals consistent with the aims and objectives of "Trees for Tomorrow". For a plan to be approved, he says, it must be:

1. ecologically sound—that is, increase BC's carbon sink through urban afforestation;
2. socially engaging—that is, demonstrate a commitment of support and involvement of community members;
3. spatially proficient—that is, transform spaces into areas where residents can be active; and
4. sustainable—that is, show a capacity for stewardship, management and long-term sustainability of project.

In addition, they must have positive, measurable impacts on the urban forest, contribute to energy savings in communities (economic objective), and generate awareness within the community about the values and the long-term benefits of urban greenery (educational component). Other requirements are that they must show linkages to other Provincial initiatives (such as ActNow BC, BC 150 celebrations, and LiveSmart BC Green Cities Awards) and have an effective communication strategy (which includes appropriate profile for all supportive partners and stakeholders on promotional items, interpretive site signage, and other materials). Running through the application checklist, Tim carefully reads out the requirements, which include:

• A draft plan for the proposed project site, including a management plan.
• A certification form or letter verifying the accuracy of the application;
• Letters of support from project partners, including funding, in-kind and volunteer commitments;
• A letter of permission from eligible applicant (for partner applicant only);
• Proposed project budget; and
• A management project timeline.

As Mr. Part continues to expound on the technical details of the application requirements, it becomes increasingly clear from the look of his listeners that he would have to revisit some of the issues to provide further explanation or justifications.

Tim's audience, numbering about fifteen, is small but diverse. They come from different communities and organizations, and are here in different capacities. They include individuals, representatives from First Nations communities, parents, teachers, school heads, regional and municipal government staff, corporate organizations, community groups and environmental stewardship organizations from the Metro Vancouver Region. The workshop serves as a forum for them to meet with one another, share concerns, build networks, and discuss ideas and partnership possibilities for projects.

During the question time, which precedes the brainstorming session, they raise a number of concerns for Mr. Part to elucidate. For example, a community member wants to know why the Province is financing 50% the project cost, not all. Mr. Part explains that the rationale is to encourage inputs from all segments of the society towards a common and worthy cause that yield beneficial gains to the whole society, and not just the government of the province. He stresses that, "as a society, it is important we all identify with our challenges and mobilize our collective strengths to address these, utilizing our individual gifts and talents in a process that engenders a sense of responsibility, togetherness and pride, which has been the hallmark of most Canadian communities. And Trees for Tomorrow is a cooperative initiative that aims to bring together government, community groups, neighbor-hoods and individuals across BC. in urban afforestation opportunities". Other questions are asked on the requirements of projects, and Mr. Part makes every effort to respond. Sometimes, however, he allows members of his team to either respond to a question or add extra comments to a response.

After a short break, Mr. Part asks participants to form discussion groups, where he and his team facilitate discussions on the various components of planning and applying for a successful project. This helps participants to understand concepts and articulate their own vision and ideas for their sites; what type of project would best suit their environments; who they must involve in the planning; and where they can mobilize additional resources.

Others include creating awareness about the environmental, social and economic values of afforestation and long-term benefits of an urban forest, mobilizing human and material resources, consulting expertise advise, identifying and establishing possible partners, defining roles of community and partners, preparing budget and management strategies, and securing, writing and submitting documentation. At this session, Mr. Part and his team are able to respond to additional questions from participants and assist them to thoroughly go through the requirements of a grant application.

Rounding up the event after the brainstorming session, Tim assures his participants that Evergreen is willing to provide any technical support, including how to start and develop community-based environmental initiatives, design projects, plan site, and provide advice on where to find helpful resources and additional funding, as well as completing a successful application, if contacted by an applicant. He warmly thanks his audience and support team on behalf of Evergreen Vancouver and himself for their presence, questions and inputs into the program and expresses his hope that participants will spread the news to their friends, families, communities and the institutions they came to represent. He also encourages them to start mobilizing themselves and putting ideas together for successful 'Trees for tomorrow" projects where they live, work and any other public spaces of interest. Tim then asks the participants, who respond with applause, to complete an evaluation form on the workshop in order to help Evergreen assess the effectiveness of the workshop and incorporate their suggestions into subsequent ones.

At the close of the workshop around 4:10pm, the first person I shake hands with is Mr. Part himself, who in response mentions my name and introduces himself to me, while he and his team pack the equipment and materials they had used at the event. Tim's acceptance of my offer to assist gives me the first-hand opportunity to acquaint myself with his work and his organization, and in turn introduce myself and the details of my mission. He tells me today has been a busy day for him and his team. They had spent the first half of the day in Richmond providing field support to the staff of an insurance corporation holding an annual meeting to plant trees at the Iona Beach Regional Park, as part of their corporate social responsibility. However, he adds that the activity is not related to Trees for Tomorrow, sensing the likelihood of me merging the two projects into one. According to him, the tree-planting exercise falls under a separate program run by his organization known as *Common Grounds*. Sensitive to his exhausted outlook, which I suppose isn't different from mine, I do not probe further, but express my keen interest in getting to know more about his profession. Before I depart, Tim tells me he will be in the office tomorrow afternoon and will be glad to have me around to continue with my exercise. He also adds that there will be a planning meeting at the office which might interest me. I respond positively and express my gratitude to Mr. Part for his reception and depart for home.

Day 2: Friday November 28, 2008
Articulating a Major Panning Challenge

The next day, I find myself in Evergreen's Office located at 555 Great Northern Way, Vancouver. This is the place where Mr. Part works. It's a small grey-painted building interspersed with green, connoting the kind of work done by its occupants. Evergreen had moved into this new building from their previous location inside an office tower at Gas town for both space and security reasons—Mr. Part later tells me.

After being welcomed into the building by a lady who I remember meeting yesterday at the workshop, she informs me of Tim's absence from the office for an appointment, but assures me that he would return in the afternoon. She then joins her two colleagues to continue their round table discussion. Suspecting that Tim might have forgotten to inform them about my interest in their discussion to understand why they do not invite me to join, I remain quiet but maintain active eyes and ears to pick any meaningful information relevant to my mission.

The first items I fix my eyes on are the huge wooden panels containing words and photos that describe the mission and activities of Evergreen. Then after, I locate a set of prestigious awards sitting on a table close to the entrance. These awards have been presented to Evergreen for their contribution to the wellbeing of communities and the environment. They come from partners, including corporate organizations and community groups. And the latest I see is from the Citizens Bank of Canada, which was presented to Evergreen in 2007, in appreciation for their contribution to the Burnside George Community Centre.

Initially unnoticed, I spot a gentleman seated at the back of the room screened from me by a glass partition. He is the director of Evergreen Vancouver Office, I am later told by Mr. Part. However, he is the technical head of Mr. Part under Evergreen's complicated administrative arrangement. Tim's actual boss, he tells me, is at the head office in Toronto, but he must report management and administrative issues to his Vancouver Director.

The three ladies working are apparently planning the next "Trees for Tomorrow" public outreach. Two of them are permanent administrative staff of Evergreen, but the third is a consultant recently contracted by the organization to manage the "Trees for Tomorrow" program on behalf of Evergreen, as Tim later explains that Evergreen hired her services to m.administer this new program because of the huge workload on him and the remaining limited staff. Among other things, I hear them discuss the ingredients of project planning as they had done the previous day. One of them highlights the importance of clearly explaining these technical words to the public in clear and unambiguous language. For instance, explaining the term visioning as a community's aspiration for space and balancing environmental goals with social needs means to ensure that tress are planted in way that allows children to play and learn under shade. Another reiterates the importance of using visual aids in the workshops to facilitate participants' understanding of concepts. Satisfactory remarks are made by each one, and the meeting closes at 1:15pm, with the new program manager, who chaired it, promising to send everyone the notes from the discussion before the next meeting, which Tim and his boss will be attending.

At about 3:37pm, Tim returns to the office, almost two and half hours after the close of the meeting, to find me, two staff and the Director. He had also been at a meeting with some municipal staff to discuss some projects. After apologizing to me for being late, he greets his boss and subordinates, and heads on to put down the box he is holding. After briefing his boss on the outcome of the meeting in a very informal style, he then dashes to his desk to check the number of calls and emails he had missed while being away. This takes less than ten minutes. Tim goes out again to bring other items from his vehicle into the office. Seeing this recur compels me to assist him, and once again that inevitably helps me to receive some briefing from Tim without asking—a way I find useful to get the best out of the little time at his disposal. Finishing with the packing of the items except the implements and tents takes us to about 4:10pm, and at this time it's only left with Tim's boss and one administrative staff. I decide not to ask this man the set of questions I intended asking him, given that the condition I find him isn't different from that of the previous encounter. But since Tim tells me he has to empty his troubled vehicle of the all the mechanical equipment into Evergreen's hired store room a few blocks away which is also close to the nearest sky train station, I respond to his offer of a ride, knowing that this will present me another opportunity—somewhat

different from the earlier ones—to slip out one of the questions stored in mind for this hard-to-capture gentleman.

On the way, I ask Tim to tell me more about his Common Grounds Program and share some of his experiences working with communities. He begins by telling me that Common Grounds is an environmental program that brings ecological restoration projects to communities. He explains that common grounds refer to spaces in communities and in cities co-shared by people as well as the flora and fauna in our local ecosystems. They include pathways, parks, playing fields and tennis courts. His activities bring together people to share a vision for those spaces that addresses key environment and community development needs. Owing to issues of land ownership, cost and the far-reaching impacts of the projects, Tim identifies, consults, and works with a number of partners, including land owners (city or municipal governments), donor organizations, youth groups, local artists, and community leaders among others in the design and implementation of projects that are creative and context appropriate". Continuing, Tim adds that "we also work with community groups and other social organizations to promote sustainable use of the spaces through diverse social activities that include community mapping, games, festivals and storytelling. This is how we contribute to making communities and cities more livable". "That sounds interesting!", I remark. "And who manages these projects after their implementation?", I ask Tim, as my closing question for the day. "Well, that's an interesting question, Komiete!", He replies.

"We encourage communities to take active responsibility for the maintenance and management of these projects, but this has been a difficult goal for Evergreen to achieve. Some have been successful through stewardship groups, but some projects have been left without any strong community-based commitment towards their management and sustainability. I think this is where we need Planners like you to help us with long-term planning of projects", Tim adds. I smile in response and indicate to him that we'll discuss the issue when I come over to the office for the concluding session of my exercise. Mr. Part and I shake hands, and within the next two minutes I'm seated in the Millennium Line sky train bound for Lougheed where I live.

DAY 3: Friday 5 December, 2008
Respect for Moral Authority; Unveiling of Professional Identity

On the last day of my adventure with Part (he had told me that he will be spending the whole working day in the office), I brace myself for an interesting time there. After reporting in at about 9:07am, Tim attends to his routine bureaucratic activities, which include checking and responding to emails, making telephone calls and appending his signature on official documents. He then has to prepare for an important meeting which will be taking place in his office for the next three hours. It is an end-of-year meeting for the Greater Vancouver Invasive Plant Council. The Greater Vancouver Invasive Plant Council (GVIPC) is a non-profit society that works with individuals, organizations and municipalities to manage invasive plants in the Greater Vancouver Region.

Members of the GVIPC include regional and municipal governments, environmental stewardship groups, academic institutions, nurseries, and non-profit organizations. The council's mandate include carrying out research and providing information and advice on the management of invasive plants to individuals and organizations, both public and private, which undertake environmental initiatives dealing with invasive plants—plants not native to the region's environment. Tim is Evergreen's representative on this body, contributing to its growth and benefiting from its research activities. Because of their so-called harmful effects on native plants and wildlife habitat, which Mr. Part tends to create or protect through his projects, he relies on the council for new information and advice on how to deal effectively with the diverse invasive plant species. Similarly, Tim provides the Council with new problems and challenges he encounters on the ground, so they could do further investigations.

The meeting begins at about 9:30am with eight members in attendance, comprising four males and four females. Being an end-of-year meeting, the agenda include a review of the programs and activities for 2008, planning for 2009, as we all other items. During the discussion, an important issue crops up that is debated by the body for some time. Considering the passion with which members air their views, it seems to me that it is an issue that has been on the table for some time without a definite conclusion or consensus been reached. A member wanted the body to consider adding field activities to their operations in order to reinforce their concerns on the ground by tackling in particular the damaging effects of invasive plant growth in some ecologically sensitive areas such as watersheds, river banks and fish ponds. Many suggestions support the idea as being worth-while, since the problem was not receiving any serious attention. However, this receives a strong opposition from another member, who happens to be the oldest on the council and a retired academic. He argues that the council was primarily established to conduct research and disseminate scientific information on invasive plants to institutions and individuals through outreach and collaboration; therefore, any field activity will constitute a constitutional breach. In addition to the possible risk of legal suit, he also cautions that the absence of an insurance cover for the council will be consequential for any field-related accident, should that occur during a field exercise. When Mr. Part is asked for his opinion, he points out that he thinks the proposal is a good for its beneficial outcomes; however if it generates many legal and financial implications, then the council may have to give consideration to those issues. The middle-aged Council chairman decides to place the issue on hold without asking members to vote on it. He, however, encourages members to deliberate over the issue and then slips in other equally important matters meant for discussion for the day. This includes recruiting new members to join the body to reflect the breadth of issues and people it deals with. On this, Tim suggests the inclusion of a working academic from one of BC's science-based post-secondary institutions, a First Nation and a transgender. All members of

the council welcome this suggestion, and ideas are put forward on the various means for attracting those people. Within the next five minutes, the two-and-half-hour meeting is brought to an end, after the Chairman's closing remarks. The closure of the meeting frees members to respond to Tim's request for their ideas on the proposed landscape design he plans to implement on the stretch of land fronting Evergreens new office. The satisfactory feedback Tim receives on his proposal for which he expresses much appreciation gives him the confidence to proceed with the implementation of his plan.

When everybody leaves, Tim and I go back into the office where he spends about ten minutes at his desk checking and sending out emails. When he's done, Mr. Part then joins me for the final session of my three-day visit, which takes the form of an interview. At is this session, Tim takes time to connect all the scattered bits of information he had given me about himself, his organization, and his experience working with communities. The following is the record of the proceeding.

Question: What is the history of Evergreen?

Response: Well, Evergreen is a national charity non-profit environmental organization founded in 1991 in Toronto to deepen the connection between people and nature and empowering Canadians to take a hands-on approach to their urban environments. The Vancouver Regional Office was set up two years later. Our mandate is to bring nature into our cities through naturalization projects. Our organization moti-vates people to create and sustain healthy, natural outdoor spaces, and gives them the practical tools to be successful.

Question: How do you deliver your services?

Response: Well, essentially we do that through two major program streams: Learning Grounds and Common Grounds. Learning Grounds is about transforming school grounds and Common Grounds conserves publicly accessible land. Apart from the differences in the spatial focus of these two programs, they are managed and administered under different arrangements. I manage Common Grounds for the Lower Mainland; the manager of Learning Grounds has a different office location, but she collaborates with us.

Question: Could you mention some of the projects you undertake under Common Grounds?

Response: The core service we provide through the Common Grounds program is Environmental Stewardship, in which we under-take a number of projects such as environmental education, environmental design and planning, habitat restoration and management planning, and partnerships implementation. We also provide training and other forms of support to environmental stewardship groups to help them work with community groups, municipal governments, landowners, foundations, non-governmental organizations and the corporate sector to establish partnerships for the rest-oration and care of parks and natural areas in urban areas across the Greater Vancouver Regional District.

Question: What participatory processes do you employ in engaging communities in your projects?

Response: We undertake surveys to identify which public spaces and parks can potentially benefit from a stewardship activity and work with those communities through volunteer groups and the municipal government to plan, design and implement a particular restoration project suitable for the identified site. Where there is an existing volunteer group, we collaborate with them and provide them the necessary support and training to build their capacity to implement and manage projects on completion. But where there are no stewardship groups, we assist in creating one through volunteer activities. In planning community projects, we attempt to involve all segments of the beneficiary community, including youth groups and seniors, through consultations and discussions.

Question: Could you expound on your relationship with local governments under Common Grounds?

Response: Yes. Essentially, all public lands and parks—including play grounds, sports fields, tennis courts, pools, municipal grounds, regional parks, ravines and creeks where our activities occur are regulated by the local government. Therefore, we are legally required to obtain permission and approval for any project or activity we propose to implement on such lands from the local government body whose jurisdictional boundary covers the site in question. And we have to ensure that our proposals fit into the community development plan of the areas concerned.

Question: Could you describe some of your experiences and challenges working with diverse communities?

Response: I would say that working with diverse communities throughout the Lower Mainland for about three years has been both rewarding and challenging. I work with many communities and stewardship groups throughout the Lower Mainland, and the responses and levels of commitment are not the same. Some stewardship groups are more active than others and some communities are more receptive to our projects than others. Being Canada's most ethnically diverse province, BC's communities present both possibilities and challenges. While in some communities, our projects continue to thrive because of the high level of support from community members during the planning, implementation, management and use of restored sites, the situation is totally different in other communities. Sometimes, there are conflicts of ideas and preferences in some communities regarding the concept of naturalization and the approach to implementing it. This cuts across culture, gender, income and age. In predominantly South Asian communities such as Surrey, for example, naturalization (seen broadly as part of agriculture) is perceived as a socially degrading activity, so many residents don't get very much involved in our activities. Moreover, there are concerns about the crime-related impact of some naturalization projects such as tree planting on parks and within residential units. This is also a common concern in some communities, especially those with women, seniors and children because of safety concerns about possible criminal activities, as well as the harboring of some unwanted wildlife. Sometimes, it occurs in the form of conflicts between youth and adults over the design features of a restoration project. Often adults prefer more conventional design schemes such as planting trees in a linear machined pattern while the youth may opt for less conventional schemes.

Question: How do you manage and deal with these challenges?

Response: We do our best to address the concerns of some communities by altering some designs and also promote dialogue and consensus-building among the competing interest groups and stakeholders. In addition, we encourage communities to initiate regular outdoor activities to keep the parks active and thus secure it from invasion by harmful animals and people.

Question: Do you find yourself sometimes sympathizing towards a community concern against the government.

Response: Evergreen is a registered charity, and the laws that govern our organization does not permit us to take an advocacy position.

Question: Can you tell me more about your professional background?

Response: Basically, I hold bachelor's degree in biology from Simon Fraser University and a diploma in renewable resources technology from the British Columbia Institute of Technology's Fish, Wildlife and Recreation Management program. I have had over ten years experience in developing and leading community stewardship activities and designing volunteer-driven restoration projects. But I joined Evergreen Vancouver some three years ago.

Question: Mr. Part, where did you learn all the skills of community mobilization and facilitation?

Response: Answer: Well, it stems from passion. I started volunteering and getting involved in community mobilization at an early age, but I also learn new skills and knowledge from the people I work with including planners, scientists, consultants, and the even the communities I work with.

3. Discussion

In the ensuing section, I make the case for considering Tim Part as a planner first based on the fit between his goals, values and actions, including the nature of his work, approach to issues and challenges faced by him, and what we know about planning and planners. I then explain aspects of his knowledge and conduct from mainstream planning theories.

3.1 Why I consider Tim Part a Planner

I have several reasons to label Mr. Part a planner. Listening to him competently use many of the planning vocabulary I have spent many years acquiring in the classroom at the workshop alone on the first day is enough a proof. But because I need to convince skeptics from within, I choose to do so from a planning perspective, employing the two-fold question I asked at the beginning of the paper: What is planning and who are planners? Lastly, how do mainstream planning theories explain Mr. Part's professional work and conduct?

On What Planning is

I acknowledged at the beginning of this paper that the disputes surrounding the history of planning as well its rapidly expanding wings make it somewhat difficult to provide a singular definition that is all embracing of who planners are and what planners do. Already, numerous attempted definitions of planning have been criticized for being either too narrow or too loose, procedural or substantive inclined, scientific biased or lacking in object. My approach to dealing with this challenge is to focus on the concerns and values planners share in common as well as the implications of every planning work.

Whether working for cities or regions, in rural or urban areas, with the public or private sectors—on land use, environment, housing or transportation—planners everywhere speak a common language: fairness, equity and justice. They have a sense of commitment to social and or environment wellbeing, and invariably their words and actions directly or indirectly impact people and space. It is this welfare-driven, value-based philosophy and far-reaching consequences of professional decisions and actions that characterize planners and the work they do which informs my decision to consider Mr. Tim Part a planner. Evidence from the nature of his work, which is environmental stewardship, and his goal of making cities more livable by deepening the connection between people and nature, demonstrate Tim's belief in the dependency relationship that exists between man and his environment—the latter being a victim of man's activities and a determinant of his survival. By raising public awareness of environmental issues and engaging communities to find solutions to these, Tim articulates his concerns for the environment and the health of cities, a matter of personal and civic responsibility.

On What Planners do

Perhaps, one important distinguishing feature of planners is the fact that they pursue goals, which define an end state; and they take steps to get there, whether pre-determined or incrementally reached. Mr. Part's goal is "to make cities more livable". Related to this is the big dilemma planners' face about whose interests is/are being represented in a particular planning activity, which leads us to the issue of power dynamics and control in planning, something I will later address.

Planning is a highly interactive field, and like other planners, Tim spends much of his time working with others, including professional planners, researchers, corporate bodies, non-profit societies, movements, community-based organizations, and local citizens with a complex maze of relationships. This also has spatial implications for his daily movements, which include oscillating between communities, public spaces, municipal offices, and many more. Like many planners, Tim experiences the pressure of deadlines and tight work schedules.

Planners must be able to think in terms of spatial relationships and visualize the effects of their plans and designs. And Tim is no different: his work involves anticipating the effects of his environmental projects on spatial and social organization. For instance, if a restoration project contains a lot of recreation facilities, it intensifies social activities in an area and makes it more open. However, if it is tree dominated and less actively recreational, it gives the community a serene and quiet look, while keeping people indoors. Tim therefore considers this balance in planning with communities for his projects. And like all planners have their geographical jurisdictions in which they work, Tim's is the entire Lower Mainland of British, a region comprised of twenty five communities. The ability to communicate effectively, both orally and in writing, which Tim Part has, is a necessary planning skill.

Planners also believe in, and work for, change or improvement wherever they find themselves. Tim's naturalization projects contribute to shaping the physical and social fabric of the urban environment with some benefits. His landscaping projects give the cities and communities that benefit from his program a unique view that blends human ingenuity and nature. By acting to protect both natural and cultural landscapes, restore degraded environments, and protect spaces from pollution and degradation, Tim contributes significantly towards the cause of sustainability, climate change and energy conservation. Research conducted by McPherson and Rowan (1993) on the energy conservation potential of urban tree planting indicate that trees can be a cost-effective energy conservation measure for electricity consumption. A single 25-ft tall tree reduces annual heating and cooling costs of a typical residence by 8 to 12 percent ($10-25); therefore, one can envisage the contributions being made by Tim towards energy savings.

Tim's community-based approach to dealing with the sustainability challenge also exemplifies how complex global and national challenges can effectively be addressed at the local level, validating the famous planning philosophy of change: that transformation occurs at the grassroots level, when ordinary people are given the necessary support to engage their skills and abilities in creative ways. By involving community members in the planning and implementation of naturalization projects through local associations, Tim recognizes the asset base of communities and creates avenues for local energies to be channeled into productive and rewarding ways. Tim's programs also contribute to community-building and social capital mobilization. It strengthens community ties by fostering a sense of cooperation and instilling feelings of pride and stewardship.

In a multicultural society like Canada where social relations are weak, Tim's stewardship programs help to bridge cultural barriers among strangers and promote co-existence among neighbors through the mix of community gardening and park maintenance activities as well as cultural events such as festivals and storytelling. This helps to ease tensions, reduce crime, substance abuse and vices associated with isolation, thereby contributing to social sustainability. His mentorship relations with

many youth groups provide them with skills and training in environ-mental stewardship, valuable knowledge and leadership capabilities. Creating and maintaining natural outdoor spaces also provides an excellent opportunity to observe, participate, learn, and enjoy a changing, complex environment. And improving societal attitudes and behaviors toward the environment begins by establishing an opportunity for regular and positive contact with the natural world.

On this basis of the nature of his work, interests, challenges, engagement with multiple stakeholders, and contributions to community-building, I consider Mr. Part an environmental planner, with social and community development expertise.

3.2 Situating Tim's Actions within Mainstream Planning Theory

Even though there is still no definitive body of theories that guide and inform planning work, the key theoretical models recognized in the planning literature are reflected in Mr. Part's work that merit our attention.

As a Rational Planner

A product of enlightenment epistemology, rational or comprehensive planning, which has an underlying faith in "solving" problems through reason and scientific methodology, is characterized by instrumental rationality in analysis and decision-making process. This process involves problem definition; determination of possible solutions; forecasting of outcomes from the solutions; evaluation of the alternatives according to chosen criteria; and implementing the best solution (Sandercock, 1998; Stiftel, 2002).

Coming from a scientific background in biology and wildlife management, Tim often finds himself surveying community environmental needs and problems, analyzing and designing comprehensive schemes to address them. As we can see from his strong attachment to the Invasive Plant Council, Tim employs a lot of 'objective' scientific knowledge in the design of his naturalization projects. And even though he involves communities in an interactive social process, they are often limited to choosing options that are presented to them by him or are feasible in his eyes. By administering the Trees for Tomorrow program on behalf of a political authority—in this context, the Government of British Columbia, Tim must ensure that applications submitted for funding conform to the policies set by politicians at the Province, expressed in terms of goals, project streams, eligibility requirements, and application procedures. Besides, all the naturalization projects he implements under his Common Grounds program must be subject to the approval of the land use policies and Official Community Plans of the various municipalities he works in. The major political ambition of the government—whether provincial, regional or municipal—is, I think, to maintain British Columbia's external reputation for being a leader in climate change efforts in Canada and globally, with its major city, Vancouver, being acclaimed one of the most livable cities in the world.

Invariably, though not a political servant, Tim would hardly escape Faludi's (1986) and Sander-cock's (1995) description of planners in this model acting as "handmaidens to power", serving political objectives, without asking who is in control and with what consequences.

Attempting to Advocate

Emerging as the first serious challenge to the rationale comprehensive model, the concept of advocacy planning seeks to represent and incorporate the needs and concerns of the unrepresented in planning decisions arrived through rational analysis and scientific objectivity (Sandercock, 1995).

Tim could be seen as an advocate who champions the environmental factor in urban growth development and policies, while promoting community involvement in environmental initiatives, planning and management. This is evident by his informing and educating the public on environmental issues, as seen in, for example, the Trees for Tomorrow Program workshop I attended and his working out naturalization projects with ordinary citizens under his Common Grounds program. Tim takes advantage of his contact with municipal authorities to voice the concerns of his organization and the communities he works with for incorporation into environmental policies.

But perhaps to the disappointment of many advocacy planners, Tim does not have the real power to make significant alterations in the policy arena; nor is he able to offer his communities the real power to influence decisions on their own, partly due to constraints imposed on him by the political rules of engagement with government, which prohibits his organization from supporting a cause against the state. Therefore, by bringing people to participate in naturalization and ecological restoration programs without offering them the tools to effect real changes on environmental policies, Tim has in a sense become what Robert Goodman describes as a 'soft cop'. Being confident in the existing democratic processes in preparing development plans, his work is, perhaps, no more than an expansion of a professional role in planning, which engages citizens in projects, while leaving the existing power structure intact.

Learning to Transact, Learn and Communicate

Transactive planning model represents a shift from expert-driven knowledge in planning to a process of mutual learning where planners engage in dialogue and develop transactive relationships with the communities they work with, to share knowledge, solve problems and resolve conflicts. This is based on the acknowledgment of, and belief in, the value of local or experiential knowledge to planning as opposed to expertise monopoly that characterizes the rational model (Sandercock, 1998). The implication is that planning becomes less a document-oriented and anticipatory approach to a process of social and mutual learning towards reaching a desirable solution.

During our interactive session, Tim shared an experience he had in one of the communities he works with that has led to a shift towards this approach to planning. According to him, he entered the community with the intention of getting people involved in the restoration of a community park, with tree planting as the major component. But through contact with the community, he realized that local citizens opposed the idea for the reason that it will contribute to increased crime and social disintegration. To them, criminals can hide behind trees which obstruct visibility to attack people at night and also make the already idle park unsafe for use. When Tim learned about this truth, he was very much astonished. But he also knew the potential of restoration activities in community building and crime reduction, when communities assume greater responsibility for the ownership, management and active use of their parks. Therefore, he had to dialogue with the community through a series of consultations to arrive at a consensus that currently sees restoration activities focused on gardening, beautification, maintenance and management, which are intermarried with festivals, games and other social events that promote integration and community building.

In the above example, Tim could be seen as a transactive planner or social learner, mediating between the interest of his organization and the community in a democratic atmosphere that combines his expertise knowledge and the experiential knowledge of the communities he works with to achieve mutual goals. Similar examples are seen in the way Tim handles multiple interests, ideas and concerns expressed in a particular community on a proposed naturalization project. Therefore, Tim tells me that incorporating local knowledge and partnership-building constitute a key component of his engagement with communities. Yet, as rightly observed by some scholars, he hardly escapes the challenges of participation which include delays, high cost and non-involvement by segments of the population.

The communicative planning model, a further development on the interactive perspective of planning, focuses on the communication strategies of planners that complement their technical work to seek and understand the interplay of their personal philosophies and the contextual environment that shape their responses (Sandercock, 1995; Stiftel, 2000). The focus is on speech acts, and the relationship between knowledge and power, through an observation of what planners do. Perhaps, this is the most visible and less structured planning theory evident from my narrative of Mr. Part's work.

Mr. Part displays different kinds of knowledge in his professional work. This includes both procedural knowledge of political institutional set-up, administrative and legal processes. At the workshop, Tim explained to participants the limits set by formal procedures in the Tree for Tomorrow grant application. Besides having knowledge about them, there is evidence that he also knows how to work his way through them, when at the end of the workshop he asked participants to freely contact his organization for technical assistance on areas, including how to complete a successful application. During my interview with him on the last day, he also demonstrated his knowledge of legal processes, which include who to contact at municipal offices for specific information and how to submit an application for permission to implement a restoration project on a municipal park. Tim also exhibited some procedural knowledge in environmental planning, when he told me that his projects often begins with surveys, design, community consultation and implementation.

Besides these procedural knowledge forms, Tim is also rich in substantive areas such as biology, ecology, renewable resources, wildlife management, environmental designs, land use, recreation management and economics. His presentation at the workshop required an ability to interpret to participants the relationship between tree planting, energy savings, income generation and climate change. And he was skilled in explaining these connections to his participants in less technical language. Tim also has rich knowledge of dealing with multiple interests, including communities, governments, corporate organizations as well as other non-profit organizations such as the Lower Mainland Invasive Plant Council, and how to meet and balance them cleverly in a single project. He is also familiar with the demographic, social and cultural structure of the different communities he works with and appreciates the different challenges posed to him in different situations. His change of tactic to engage the community that opposed his tree-dominated restoration design to work out a solution that addresses the concerns of the community yet meets his organization's interest shows how proactive Tim is, when faced with conflicts of interest.

Tim's explanation of the eligibility requirements for the Trees for Tomorrow grant application is a demonstration of his understanding of the various standards required by the BC Government for any proposed project, just as he ensures that his restoration plans conform to the existing plans of the various municipalities he works. By linking his activities to community building and social mobilization, Tim demonstrates his understanding of environmental and social interrelationships inherent to the urban fabric. The way Tim responded to the question on why the BC government is funding up to half the cost of approved projects under Trees for Tomorrow at the workshop shows how he can invoke moral value to interpret decisions. In explaining why procedures must be followed and referring participants to other sources of knowledge about the Tress for Tomorrow application procedures, Tim also exemplifies the principle that the expert committed to democratic delivery of expertise should not only inform but also provide adequate reasons to allow knowledge to be validated or checked out.

Tim structured the agenda for the workshop using the power conferred on him as the presenter, as he moved from one stage to the other during the event: introduction, presentation, question time, brainstorming session (which guided by him and his team members), evaluation and closure. Concurrently, he was also constrained by the requirements set for the program by the BC Government. In the third episode, the discussions that took place at the council meeting followed the agenda set by the council chairman which Tim had to comply with under the device of formality. During the discussions, Tim was clearly dominated by the opinion of the senior council member, whose strong opposition to the proposal overshadowed his response that "he thinks the proposal is a good for its beneficial outcomes; however if it generates many legal and financial implications, then the council may have to give consideration to those issues". In this context, the senior used the constitution of the body to justify his opposition which Tim had to oblige, even though he thought the suggestion was good.

The use of technology is a relatively new area now gaining traction in planning attention. In this context, Tim's use of PowerPoint aided his audience to validate what he says with what is written and a backup for things not properly understood or explained verbally. The use of visual aid during the presentation helped participants to better appreciate certain concepts. Tim also relied on feedback as a means of externally validating both his performance and the relevance of the workshop, as a democratic practitioner subjecting himself to scrutiny.

In all three episodes, Tim was surrounded by constraints of different types that appeared to shape his actions. These include his work environment (physical, social and ethical). From my observation, Tim's working environment was conducive for him, as he relates well with his Director and other administrative staff. Other external constraints imposed on him are the ethical laws governing his organization which determines the boundaries of his acts when dealing with communities and bureaucratic political structures. Also, because his organization has been contracted by a political authority to administer the Trees for Tomorrow Program, he is confined to 'defend' the government in all matters relating to policy and procedures.

In his daily work, Tim deployed sophisticated knowledge and communicative skills informed by professional knowledge and values, personal principles, and a wealth of experience.

Traits of Radicalism

Radical planning practices emerged from a critique of planning as elitist, centralizing, change-resistant and male-dominated, and proposed a new paradigm based upon systems change, decentralization, communal society, facilitation of human development and empowerment, with the focus depending on the nature of the critique.

Even though Tim's stewardship projects, in which he mobilizes local communities through volunteering and equips them to take a hands-on approach to manage their urban environment may not be oppositional to the state, as is typical of radical planning practice, it imbibes certain traits of radicalism. But motivating people and mobilizing communities to create and sustain healthy, natural outdoor spaces and giving them the practical tools required, Tim can be said to be practicing radical planning. Indeed, if Tim's Common Grounds projects strengthen community ties by fostering a sense of cooperation and instilling feelings of pride and stewardship, which builds a sense of individual empowerment – in that people learn that they can make a difference to the health of their community and the environment - who would not describe him as a radical planner? The basic argument here is that, through his activities, Tim is making local folks less dependent on the state bureaucracies responsible for panning their green spaces,

even though he maintains contact with the appropriate political authorities to ensure conformity. This later fact confirms Sandercock's assertion that "while it may be a contradiction in terms to think of the state engaging in radical planning, it is equally misleading to think that radical planning can do without the state" (Sandercock 1998: 101). But what about his allegiance? Is it to the state or to the communities? Well, in this context, I see Tim being sympathetic to the cause of communities, though not loyal to them, but avoiding conflict with the state.

In summary, Tim can be described as pragmatic technician, employing tools and objective knowledge to solve problems; as an advocate, representing the needs of the environment and local communities in local policies; as a promoter of change, dialoging and collaborating with local communities through shared knowledge; as a communicator, sensitive to his circumstances and interacting with power dynamics; and as a mobilizer, rallying and empowering his communities to take charge of their environments.

4. Implications and Conclusion

The above piece, which is a deliberation on the major identity issue in planning, has shown how the shift from traditional notions of planning as the means of allocating land, resources and facilities for welfare enhancement and progress, to dealing with the broader social, political, economic, environmental issues impacting or being impacted by traditional planning practices. Inevitably, this has contributed to putting the profession in a dilemma, as the so-called critical issues contemporary planning deals with belong to other disciplines with well-defined professional identities from which planning borrows knowledge. A direct implication of the shift in the focus of planning work today is that, unlike other traditional disciplines such as architecture, geography and economics, modern day planning lacks the authority to definitively demarcate its boundaries in way that is precise for defining who is, or can be labeled, a planner, without being subject to contestations. The other implication is that, contrary to the perception held by many products of planning school, planners are not "self-sufficient" in knowledge.

And the import of these is that the profession must be flexible and willing to embrace new paradigms and knowledge frontiers, as well as accept other professionals engaged in various planning work such as Tim Part, who may not be products of planning schools. And like Tim Part, these professionals perform very important roles and posses a rich wealth of knowledge and skills, including but not limited to community development, grassroots organizing, participatory planning, project design, communication and political decision-making processes—competencies which are considered fundamental to successful planning practice. They also, in a variety ways, are contributing to social empowerment, inclusivity, equity and change, which constitute planning's core values and goals. And, as we have seen from the story of Tim Part, the everyday challenges encountered by these professionals, such as apathy, resource constraints, conflicting interest and lack of long-term beneficiary commitment to

post-implementation management of project or programs; and the means they adopt to deal with these challenges, including awareness creation and finding creative ways to encourage local involvement in decision-making and projects, diversify funding streams and resolve conflicts, do not differentiate them from professionally-trained planners. Should the planning profession, then, dispose off its traditional identity and become what everyone makes of it? Should it be open to any Dick, Tom and Harry who claims to have some planning knowledge, skills and experience, to call themselves planners, without having any appreciation of the historical and internal ideological struggle surrounding the profession (that is to say, knowledge of planning history and theory)? And, if so, isn't planning poised to become a vague and irrelevant profession in our world?, confirming Wildvasky's famous 1973 assertion that "if planning is everything, maybe it's nothing"

To the contrary not. Planning, as we know and have seen, is, despite its "identity crisis" and internal battles, becoming more and more relevant in our fast-urbanizing and multicultural world, confronted by the multi-dimensional challenges of climate change, social inequality, exclusion, racial misunderstanding, insecurity, and resource scarcity of unprecedented scale—challenges that require the input of planners ever than before. But while it is laudable and practical, in my view, for planning to be embracive of other professionals who bring other forms of knowledge and experience to enrich the profession, it must, at the same time, clearly define, project and defend its core values as well as have an enforceable professional ethics which not only sets it apart from any other profession, but are also embraced by those wishing to wear the professional hat. I consider my experience with Mr. Part insightful and perhaps sobering; and yet, it reinforces my own opinions about planning.

References

Faludi, Andreas. 1986. Critical Rationalism and Planning Methodology. London. Pion.

Government of British Columbia. 2008 'Province Launches Trees for Tomorrow'. News Release (Sep. 25). Accessed from http://www2.news.gov.bc. ca/news_releases2005-2009/2008CD 0104-001449.htm

Healey, Patsy. 1992. 'A Planner's Day. Knowledge and Action in Communicative Practice'. *Journal of the American Planning Association*, vol. 58. no. 1, Winter.

Hodge, Gerald. 2005. Planning Canadian Communities: An introduction to the Principles, Practice, and Participants. Scarborough: Nelson, 5th edition.

Sandercock, Leonie. 1998. "The Difference that Theory Makes." Pp. 85-104 in Towards Cosmopolis: Planning for Multicultural Cities. John Wiley and Sons.

Shiftel, Bruce. 2000. 'Planning Theory'. The National AICP Exam Preparation Course Guidebook. Washington, DC. APA Press. Accessed from http://www.coa.gatech.edu/~stiftel/STIFTE L_AICP_Planning_Theory_Chapter.pdf